Sanctification in the New Testament

SANCTIFICATION
in the New Testament

by
Ralph Earle

Beacon Hill Press of Kansas City
Kansas City, Missouri

Permission to quote from the following copyrighted versions of the Bible is acknowledged with appreciation:

The Holy Bible, New International Version (NIV), copyright © 1973, 1978, 1984 by the International Bible Society.

New American Standard Bible (NASB), © The Lockman Foundation, 1960, 1962, 1963, 1968, 1971, 1972, 1973, 1975, 1977.

KJV—King James Version

Unless otherwise indicated, all Scripture quotations are from the NIV.

10 9 8 7 6 5 4 3 2

Contents

Foreword   7

Preface   9

BIBLICAL OVERVIEW

1. **Matthew**   13
   • Baptism with the Holy Spirit (3:11) • The Pure in Heart (5:8) • The Cost of Discipleship (16:24)

2. **Acts**   16
   • Pentecost (1:5, 8; 2:1-11) • The Samaritan Revival (8:5, 14-17)

3. **Romans**   22
   • Sanctification Through Death to Self (c. 6) • The Need for Sanctification (c. 7) • Sanctification Through the Spirit (c. 8)

4. **1 Corinthians**   25
   • Spiritual Gifts (c. 12) • Speaking in Tongues (c. 14)

SERMONS

5. **Galatians**   29
   "Let Me Die!" (2:20; 3:1-3; 5:16-25)

6. **Ephesians**   38
   "The Holy Church" (1:3, 13-14; 4:30; 5:25-33)

7. **1 Thessalonians**   44
   "Sanctification: The Will of God" (1:4-10; 3:12—4:7; 5:23-24)

8. **Hebrews**   52
   "The Perseverance of the Saints" (12:1-3, 14)

9. **1 Peter**   60
   "What Is a Holy Person?" (1:15-16)

10. **1 John**   67
    "Walking in the Light" (1:7; 4:7-21)

Foreword

Ralph Earle, a scholar known and read throughout world Christianity, is really at heart a gospel preacher of depth and simplicity. This comes through beautifully in this latest book, *Sanctification in the New Testament.* A lifetime in the classroom has served to spur him on to explain with great clarity and effectiveness the work of the Holy Spirit in practical terms. During those years in the classroom he balanced his ministry with consistent pulpit work in camp meetings, revivals, and conventions. His heartbeat then and now is that people will see the light and press on to the glorious fulfillment of the experience of holiness.

His impressive record of scholarly achievements can be found elsewhere, but he leaves a record of writings, translations, and practical helps that will continue to instruct and bless the followers of Christ for many decades to come.

Sanctification in the New Testament lifts up some of the outstanding biblical passages on holiness from which Dr. Earle draws spiritual holiness lessons. How to have a holy church or a holy life is a subject for intense scrutiny.

This small book is the essence of practical, biblical holiness compressed into a few simply-stated chapters. Every page is filled with meaning easily understood by the reader. As he has done in hundreds of camp meetings and local church revivals, Dr. Earle explains the way more perfectly.

RAYMOND W. HURN

Preface

In the spring of 1986 I was asked to teach three weeks at the Seminario Nazareno Mexicano, outside Mexico City. I suggested to Dr. Honorato Reza, the founding president, that I might give a course on "Sanctification in Paul's Epistles." Then I recalled that in 1940 I wrote my doctoral dissertation in Boston on "The Doctrine of Sanctification in the New Testament." So I broadened the subject of my seminary course to "Sanctification in the New Testament," the title of this book.

At the end of the second week, as we came to the close of the last session on Friday, I sensed that the Holy Spirit was moving in the hearts of some of the students. Asking them all to close their eyes, I said, "Is there someone here who feels that you need to be sanctified?"

Several hands were raised. We went to our knees in prayer, and soon five students prayed through to clear victory. In the classroom I had not only delineated the doctrine but also emphasized the experience.

Finally came the last session of the course. As it was about time to dismiss the class at twelve o'clock, a student raised his hand and asked for permission to speak. Then he stood to his feet and with vibrant voice declared: "This has been the greatest week of my life, since I was sanctified last Friday noon!" The other four who had prayed followed him with equally joyous testimonies. Then the whole class formed a circle around the room and sang several songs of thanksgiving to God. The atmosphere was electrified with the Holy Spirit's presence.

My main field of teaching over a period of 50 years (1933-83) has been New Testament, in Greek and English. Exegesis and exposition, in the classroom and pulpit, has been my vocation. In the latter place it has always ended with application and exhortation.

This book is not a theological treatise. My primary purpose and deep concern has been to help people see the light of this glorious truth of entire sanctification and receive this gracious experience.

During many years of intensive study of the Greek text I have become increasingly convinced that the New Testament teaches entire sanctification as a second crisis in Christian experience. This is God's will (1 Thess. 4:3) for every born-again believer.

Back in the 18th century John Wesley was concerned about people failing to walk in the light of holiness. He wrote:

> I am not afraid that the people called Methodists should ever cease to exist either in Europe or America. But I am afraid, lest they should only exist as a dead sect, having the form of religion without the power. And this undoubtedly will be the case, unless they hold fast both the doctrine, spirit, and discipline with which they first set out. (*Works,* Thomas Jackson edition, 13:258)

Two hundred years later it has been acknowledged in England that there are more Muslims than Methodists in the land of the Wesleys. God forbid that a similar fate should overtake the holiness movement in the United States!

Shortly before Dr. J. B. Chapman died he was asked, "Do you think the day will ever come when the Church of the Nazarene will cease to teach and preach old-fashioned, second blessing holiness?"

His reply was, "No." But then, with tears streaming down his face, he added: "The thing I fear is that the time will come when our people will have the theory but not possess the experience." This is strikingly similar to what John Wesley said, as quoted above.

What was Dr. Chapman's own position on the subject of sanctification? In his book *Holiness, the Heart of Christian Experience* (p. 10) he wrote: "Regeneration and entire sanctification are the two crises in which God deals with the sin problem in us and by which He takes us out of sin and then takes sin out of us." That expresses the truth very clearly. He also declared: "We have the task of bringing the people of God into the grace and blessing of Bible sanctification" (*All Out for Souls,* 7).

1

MATTHEW

1. Baptism with the Holy Spirit (3:11)

Some years ago the Church of the Nazarene was holding a General Assembly in the Civic Auditorium in downtown Kansas City. When the general superintendent in charge of the session had been graciously welcomed by a city leader, he sought to enliven the situation with a facetious remark like this: "You know, we are the oldest Christian denomination in the world. We are the Church of the *Nazarene.*" Immediately the city leader stepped forward with the counterproposal: "I'm a Baptist. We are older than you because we go back to John the Baptist." Of course everybody laughed, and the assembly got off to a pleasant start.

What did John the Baptist preach? We are all familiar with his main message: "Repent, for the kingdom of heaven is near" (Matt. 3:2). And Jesus began His messianic ministry with exactly the same text (4:17).

But too often it is forgotten that John the Baptist went on to say: "I baptize you with water for repentance. But after me will come one who is more powerful than I . . . He will baptize you with the Holy Spirit and with fire" (Matt. 3:11)—that is, with a fiery, cleansing baptism with the Holy Spirit. This is what Jesus came to bring. Mrs. C. H. Morris put it well:

There is sanctifying power,
Like a sweet, refreshing shower,
   Waiting for each consecrated heart:
Power to cleanse us from all sin,
Power to keep us pure within,
   Power for service which He will impart.

Across nearly 2,000 years of Christian history the church has given consistent emphasis to the importance of water baptism. But how much preaching has there been on the fiery baptism of the Holy Spirit that will cleanse the heart from sin? That is one of the great needs of our day.

That fire was used as a cleansing agent is illustrated in Num. 31:22-23: "Gold, silver, bronze, iron, tin, lead and anything else that can withstand fire must be put through the fire, and then it will be clean." Only fire could destroy dangerous disease germs. And the worst disease in all the universe is sin in the human heart. The only way we can be cleansed from that disease is by the baptism with the Holy Spirit and fire. Let us resound that tremendous truth today.

2. The Pure in Heart (5:8)

The Sermon on the Mount begins with eight beatitudes. The sixth one is:

> "Blessed are the pure in heart,
> for they will see God."

Who are "the pure in heart"? The great Danish philosopher Kierkegaard wrote: "Purity of heart is to will one intention." That is, the pure in heart have just one intent and desire, and that is to do the will of God. This can only be true when our hearts have been cleansed from all self-will. We no longer want our own way; we just want God's way. And only the fiery baptism of the Holy Spirit can "burn out the dross of inbred sin"—to use the words of a familiar song.

14

To the pure in heart the glorious promise is made: "For they will see God." This is often interpreted as meaning that after we leave this world we will see God. It also means that we will see Him here and now. Sin is like dust in the eyes; it beclouds our vision of God and distorts our view of Him. Only a fully cleansed heart can see God clearly.

3. The Cost of Discipleship (16:24)

Jesus said: "If anyone would come after me, he must deny himself and take up his cross and follow me."

What is self-denial? It is the opposite of self-assertion. If we are going to be Christ's disciples, we have to acknowledge that we cannot save ourselves; only He can save us. We cannot have our own way; we must let Him have His way.

And what does it mean to take up one's cross? Jesus has given us the example for this. In Gethsemane He prayed: "Not my will, but yours be done" (Luke 22:42). For Him it meant death on the Cross. And so cross-bearing means dying to self, going Jesus' way—the way of the Cross. It means saying to God: "Not my will, but yours be done."

In the Greek the verbs *deny* and *take up* are in the aorist tense, which suggests momentary action. But the verb *follow* is in the present tense of continuous action. So the verse may be taken as indicating two crises—a crucial conversion and a complete consecration—and then a continual following Christ the rest of our lives. That is the price we have to pay to be a true disciple of Jesus.

2

ACTS

1. Pentecost (1:5, 8; 2:1-11)

One of the great evangelists of the last generation was Gypsy Smith. Once he was asked: "What is the greatest need of the Church today?"

His immediate answer was: "Another Pentecost!"

The inquirer then asked: "What is the second greatest need?"

Once more the evangelist replied: "Another Pentecost!"

The questioner probed one more time by asking: "And what is the third most important need?"

Gypsy had just one answer to give: "Another Pentecost!"

We would heartily agree with his assessment. But what does "Pentecost" mean? That is what we want to investigate as we look into Acts.

Pentecost is the most important event in the Book of Acts. Without it the book would never have been written, for there would have been nothing to write.

Pentecost is the Greek word for "fifty." It is the New Testament name—adopted by the Jews in the intertestamental period—for the Old Testament "Feast of Weeks." Deut. 16:9-10 gives background: "Count off seven weeks from the time you begin to put the sickle to the standing grain. Then celebrate the Feast of Weeks to the Lord your God." After the 49-day interval, the feast took place on the 50th day. That was why it was called "Pentecost."

In Acts 1:4 Jesus told the disciples not to leave Jerusalem, "but wait for the gift my Father promised, which you have heard me speak about." What was that gift? Verse 5 tells us: "For John baptized with water, but in a few days you will be baptized with the Holy Spirit." This reminds us of John the Baptist's prediction (Matt. 3:11), which we discussed in our chapter on Matthew.

The key verse of the Book of Acts is Acts 1:8: "But you will receive power when the Holy Spirit comes on you; and you will be my witnesses in Jerusalem, and in all Judea and Samaria, and to the ends of the earth."

This verse gives both the power and program of the Church of Jesus Christ. To elaborate:

> The *power* is the Holy Spirit. The *program* is the evangelization of the world. For a person to claim to be filled with the Spirit and yet not to be vitally concerned about world missions is to deny his profession. When the Holy Spirit fills the human heart with His power and presence, He generates the urge to carry out Christ's command. The converse is also true: the Great Commission cannot be fulfilled without the power of the Spirit. (*Beacon Bible Commentary,* 7:262)

This verse also gives the three main divisions of the Book of Acts: (1) Witnessing in Jerusalem (cc. 1—7); (2) Witnessing in All Judea and Samaria (cc. 8—12); (3) Witnessing in the Gentile World (cc. 13—28). The disciples followed the program their Master had outlined for them.

What we have just noted was preliminary to the "day of Pentecost," which is described in the second chapter of Acts. We are told that the 120 in the Upper Room (1:13, 15) were "all together in one place" (2:1). They were obediently waiting for the fulfillment of Jesus' promise in Acts 1:8.

17

And then it happened! "Suddenly a sound like the blowing of a violent wind came from heaven and filled the whole house where they were sitting. They saw what seemed to be tongues of fire that separated and came to rest on each of them. All of them were filled with the Holy Spirit and began to speak in other tongues as the Spirit enabled them" (vv. 2-4).

In verses 2-4 three significant symbols accompanied the infilling with the Holy Spirit on the Day of Pentecost. The first was the roaring "sound like the blowing of a violent wind." This was a symbol of the *power* Jesus promised in Acts 1:8. The second was "tongues of fire that separated and came to rest on each of them." This was a symbol of the *purity* John the Baptist promised in Matt. 3:11. The third was the speaking "in other tongues." This was a symbol of the *propagation* of the gospel. And the central thing was that all of them "were filled with the Holy Spirit." This was the greatest miracle of Pentecost.

Have you had your personal Pentecost? The songwriter has phrased the question:

> *Have you ever felt the power*
> *Of the Pentecostal fire,*
> *Burning up all carnal nature,*
> *Cleansing out all base desire,*
> *Going thro' and thro' your spirit,*
> *Cleansing all its stain away?*
> *Oh, I'm glad, so glad to tell you*
> *It is for us all today.*

Today some who emphasize the aspect of power tend to minimize, or even eliminate, that of purity. They deny that when we are filled with the Spirit our hearts are cleansed from all sin. But when Peter was explaining at the Jerusalem Council what had happened to the people in the house of Cornelius, he asserted: "God, who knows the heart, showed

18

that he accepted them by giving the Holy Spirit to them, just as he did to us. He made no distinction between us and them, for he purified their hearts by faith" (Acts 15:8-9). That is, when they were filled with the Spirit, their hearts were "purified." Incidentally, in these two verses "them" means Gentiles and "us" means Jews. The former were to be just as much a part of the Christian church as the latter.

The use of the word *tongues* here in relation to the Day of Pentecost merits a bit of consideration. In verses 4 and 11 the Greek word is *glossais*. The singular is *glossa*, which was used first for the physical tongue in our mouth and then for what was spoken by that tongue.

But we also find in verses 6 and 8 the Greek word *dialectos*, which in that day meant "language" (Acts 1:19; 2:6, 8; 21:40; 22:2; 26:14). It is correctly translated that way in the NASB and NIV (and most versions today). (The KJV translates it as "tongue" in verse 8.)

Now it is perfectly clear that in Acts 2:4-11 the Greek words *glossa* and *dialectos* are used interchangeably as referring to the same thing. In the Upper Room the 120 disciples, when filled with the Holy Spirit, spoke in "other tongues" (v. 4). Then we are told: "Now there were staying in Jerusalem God-fearing Jews from every nation under heaven. When they heard this sound, a crowd came together in bewilderment, because each one heard them speaking in his own language" (vv. 5-6). Knowing that the speakers were *ignorant* "Galileans," the hearers asked each other: "Then how is it that each of us hears them in his own native language?" (v. 8).

There follows in verses 9-11 a list of not less than 15 language areas represented in the crowd that heard the Spirit-filled disciples speaking. In amazement the people were exclaiming, "We hear them declaring the wonders of God in our own tongues!"

No one can deny the obvious fact that the speaking "in other tongues" on the Day of Pentecost was not the use of some unknown tongues but rather the speaking clearly and intelligibly in the known languages of that time, proclaiming the gospel to those who had not heard it. And what was the result of this? Three thousand people were saved that day (v. 41).

Incidentally, some have claimed that with the crowd it was a miracle of *hearing* and not of speaking. But that idea is clearly ruled out by verse 6, where it is stated that "each one heard them speaking in his own language."

A pertinent illustration comes from a Friends district superintendent who once shared an outstanding experience in his spiritual life as a pastor.

He received a call one day to go to the hospital and share the good news of salvation with a man the doctor said would not live through the night. He sat at the bedside of this stranger and tried to converse with him. But he discovered right away that the man did not understand him at all, and neither could the pastor get what the sick man tried to say to him. They did not speak the same language.

Frustrated the pastor prayed earnestly that the Lord would enable him to explain to this dying man how he could be saved. He soon found himself conversing with the patient, who gave his heart to God. But the pastor had no idea what language they were conversing in.

My friend told me: "Sometime later I heard a Norwegian speaking, and the language sounded familiar. I checked with the hospital and found that the patient I had led to the Lord was indeed a Norwegian." That makes sense!

2. The Samaritan Revival (8:5, 14-17)

After Stephen's death by stoning because of his Christian faith (7:54-60), "a great persecution broke out against the church at Jerusalem" (8:1). Then: "Philip went down to a city in Samaria and proclaimed the Christ there" (v. 5). He performed miracles of healing (vv. 6-7), and "there was great joy in that city" (v. 8).

After some space of time there was a second phase in this Samaritan revival, as indicated in verses 14-17: "When the apostles in Jerusalem heard that Samaria had accepted the word of God, they sent Peter and John to them. When they arrived, they prayed for them that they might receive the Holy Spirit, because the Holy Spirit had not yet come upon any of them; they had simply been baptized into the name of the Lord Jesus. Then Peter and John placed their hands on them, and they received the Holy Spirit." These people in Samaria were converted to Christ through the preaching of Philip. Then at a later time they were filled with the Holy Spirit under the ministry of Peter and John. For them there were clearly two distinct spiritual experiences.

This passage does not *prove* that being filled with the Holy Spirit is definitely a second crisis in Christian experience, but it certainly fits in with this pattern. We shall find later, especially in 1 Thessalonians, clear evidence for the "two works of grace," regeneration and sanctification.

3

ROMANS

1. Outline

The Epistle to the Romans is rightly considered to be the most theological of Paul's 13 Epistles. It deals primarily with soteriology—that is, the doctrine of salvation (from *soter,* the Greek word for Savior).

The first eight chapters of the book comprise the doctrinal section. Here we find Paul discussing three doctrines: (1) Sin (1:18—3:20); (2) Justification (3:21—5:21); (3) Sanctification (cc. 6—8). It is interesting to discover that even non-Wesleyan commentators agree that chapters 6—8 deal with the subject of sanctification. So this is the section of the Epistle on which we shall concentrate our attention.

2. Sanctification Through Death to Self (c. 6)

The death of Christ on the Cross was not only to atone for our sins but also to give us deliverance from the inward nature of sin—what has popularly been called "the carnal nature." In verse 6 Paul writes: "For we know that our old self was crucified with him so that the body of sin might be done away with, that we should no longer be slaves to sin." (Incidentally, if you have the first edition of the NIV, change "ren-

22

dered powerless" to "done away with"—the official wording now.)

Paul goes on to say in verse 7: "Because anyone who has died has been freed from sin." There is widespread teaching today that we can only be "freed from sin"—that is, from the sinful nature (cleansed from all sin)—"in the hour and article of death." But Paul is teaching here, as the context (v. 6) clearly shows, that when by faith we have identified ourselves with Christ on the Cross ("our old self was crucified with him"), then "the body of sin" is "destroyed" (KJV), or "done away with" (NASB, NIV). Then we have died to sin and are "freed from sin"—what theologians call inbred sin or inherited depravity. Paul declares that we can be freed from sin in this life, not just at physical death.

In verse 10 the apostle writes of Christ: "The death he died, he died to sin once for all; but the life he lives, he lives to God." Then he adds the application to us: "In the same way, count yourselves dead to sin but alive to God in Christ Jesus" (v. 11). Obviously, we are not "dead to sin" until the sinful nature—"our old self" (v. 6) has been destroyed by being crucified with Christ. That happens when we by faith "count" ourselves "dead to sin" (v. 11).

3. The Need for Sanctification (c. 7)

In this chapter Paul first deals with life under the Mosaic law (vv. 1-16). In verse 17 he declares that when he did wrong, "It is no longer I myself who do it, but it is sin living in me." He defines this in verse 18 as "my sinful nature." In verse 20 he again calls it "sin living in me." In verses 23 and 25 he designates it "the law of sin."

Is there no hope of deliverance from this inner nature of sin? There is! In verse 24 Paul cries out: "What a wretched man I am! Who will rescue me from this body of death?" In verse 25 we have his cry of victory: "Thanks be to God— through Jesus Christ our Lord!" He can, and will, deliver us

23

from this "sinful nature" (v. 5) as we by faith identify ourselves with Him in His crucifixion, and so die to self. This is the negative side of sanctification.

4. Sanctification Through the Spirit (c. 8)

As noted previously, chapters 6 and 7 present the negative side of sanctification—through being crucified with Christ (6:6) and so becoming "dead to sin" (v. 11)—and thus being rescued from "this body of death" (7:24). Chapter 8 presents the positive side of sanctification: being filled with the Spirit.

The Holy Spirit is not mentioned in chapter 7. In striking contrast, He is named abut 20 times in chapter 8. Here we have life in the Spirit. Paul declares that "through Christ Jesus the law of the Spirit of life set me free from the law of sin and death" (v. 2). Now he could say that he did "not live according to the sinful nature but according to the Spirit" (v. 4). He warns us: "Those controlled by the sinful nature cannot please God" (v. 8).

One of the ministries of the Holy Spirit to us is that He guides and helps us in our prayer life. In verses 26 and 27 Paul writes: "In the same way, the Spirit helps us in our weakness. We do not know what we ought to pray for, but the Spirit himself intercedes for us with groans that words cannot express. And he who searches our hearts knows the mind of the Spirit, because the Spirit intercedes for the saints in accordance with God's will."

4

1 CORINTHIANS

1. Spiritual Gifts (c. 12)

Problem church? Paul had one! That is vividly shown in his First Epistle to the Corinthians. In it he deals with no less than nine problems existing in the Corinthian church. He handles these in a very straightforward, and sometimes stern, fashion.

General Superintendent R. T. Williams once said that the only way to avoid having any problems in a church was this: "Don't take in any new members and chloroform the ones you already have. Every person is a potential problem."

The main problem in the church at Corinth was that of divisions in the congregation. So Paul here says: "There are different kinds of gifts, but the same Spirit. There are different kinds of service, but the same Lord. There are different kinds of working, but the same God works all of them in all men" (vv. 4-6). The unity of the Trinity is to be reflected strongly in the unity of the Church.

Paul then proceeds, in verses 7-11, to name no less than nine gifts of the Spirit. The list ends with "different kinds of tongues" and "interpretation of tongues" (v. 10).

Another list is found in verses 27-30. Again we find "different kinds of tongues" at the very end (v. 28). The fact that this gift is at the bottom of both lists is certainly very significant. "Speaking in different kinds of tongues" was the least gift, not the most important one. And as we saw in our study of the second chapter of Acts, this could very well mean "different languages." One thing is certain: Paul did not treat the gift of tongues as an evidence that one had been filled with the Spirit. It was just one of many gifts of the Spirit, and apparently the least important.

At the very end of this chapter he makes this significant announcement: "And now I will show you the most excellent way." What was that? It was the way of love, as presented beautifully in chapter 13—the great "love chapter" in the Bible. And that chapter begins with these very significant words: "If I speak in the tongues of men and of angels, but have not love, I am only a resounding gong or a clanging cymbal."

Paul continues by saying: "If I have the gift of prophecy and can fathom all mysteries and all knowledge, and if I have a faith that can move mountains, but have not love, I am nothing. If I give all I possess to the poor, and surrender my body to the flames, but have not love, I gain nothing" (vv. 2-3).

Paul's prescription for a problem church is in these three verses. It is not eloquence, knowledge, faith, or good works— four things in which the Corinthians gloried. No; the correct prescription is *love.* That alone will solve their problems. Teresa of Avila (1515-82) said: "Our Lord does not care so much for the importance of our works as for the love with which they are done."

2. Speaking in Tongues (c. 14)

Tying into the whole emphasis of chapter 13, Paul begins chapter 14 by saying: "Follow the way of love and eagerly desire spiritual gifts, especially the gift of prophecy"—or, "preaching." In verses 2-4 the apostle points out the vast superiority of preaching over tongues-speaking. In verse 9 he warns his readers: "Unless you speak intelligible words with your tongue, how will anyone know what you are saying? You will just be speaking into the air." In verse 12 he exhorts his readers: "Since you are eager to have spiritual gifts, try to excel in gifts that build up the church."

Six times in this chapter the KJV has the expression "*unknown* tongue" (vv. 2, 4, 13, 14, 19, 27). Today *italics* are used for added emphasis. In the KJV italics are used for words that are not in the inspired Greek text. There is apparently no justification for adding "unknown."

Verse 18 is a favorite with those who emphasize speaking in tongues. Paul writes: "I thank God that I speak in tongues more than all of you." What did he mean?

Adam Clarke, the leading early Wesleyan commentator, gives this good answer:

> He understood more languages than any of them did; and this was indispensably necessary, as he was the apostle of the Gentiles in general, and had to preach to different provinces where different dialects, if not languages, were used. . . . it is very probable that he knew more languages than any man in the church of Corinth. (*Commentary on the Holy Bible,* 1-vol. ed., 1118)

This fits in perfectly with what we found in our study of the second chapter of Acts, that the speaking in tongues on the Day of Pentecost was unquestionably a speaking in the known, intelligible languages of that day. This was necessary for the effective proclamation of the gospel at that event, where the crowd included people from 15 different language areas. That, however, would not be true in the congregation at Corinth. And so Paul says: "But in the church I would rather speak five intelligible words to instruct others than ten thousand words in a tongue" (v. 19). The situation at Corinth was so bad that Paul adds this gentle(?) reproof: "Brothers, stop thinking like children. In regard to evil be infants, but in your thinking be adults" (v. 20). Good advice!

To be fair, we should perhaps acknowledge that some good commentators hold that the speaking in tongues at Corinth was a matter of ecstatic utterance. We would not rule that out. There are some matters, even of biblical interpretation, for which we will not have the final, full answers until we get to heaven.

*   *   *

The first four chapters of this book have looked into Matthew, Acts, Romans, and 1 Corinthians. The next five chapters will be in the form of sermons on outstanding passages on sanctification in Galatians, Ephesians, 1 Thessalonians, Hebrews, and 1 Peter. We hope that these sermons will preach themselves into the hearts and minds of many of our readers for their spiritual good. God grant that it may be so.

5

GALATIANS
Let Me Die!

Scripture: Gal. 2:20; 3:1-3; 5:16-25
Text: Gal. 2:20

Introduction:

Every resurrection must be preceded by a crucifixion. You can't come to Easter Sunday without going through Good Friday. That's a chronological fact, but it has theological implications. You can't reach the empty tomb unless you take the road that goes through the Garden of Gethsemane and past the Cross of Calvary. One of the great paradoxes of Christianity is simply this: You have to die to live!

I. The Crucifixion of the Carnal Self

George Mueller, that great man of faith of Bristol, England, once said: "There was a day when I died, utterly died." And on his 90th birthday he wrote these words:

> I was converted in November, 1825, but I only came into the full surrender of the heart four years later, in July, 1829. The love of money was gone, the love of place was gone, the love of position was gone, the love of worldly pleasures was gone. God, God alone became my portion.

29

He also wrote: "After I was filled with the Spirit, I learned more about the Scriptures in four hours than I had learned in the previous four years."

It should be noted that George Mueller used two expressions to describe the experience that came to him four years after his conversion. First, he called it "the full surrender of the heart." That's our part. We have to surrender our will fully to God's will. In the second place, he called it being "filled with the Spirit." That's God's part. God made us with free wills; so He can't compel us to surrender our wills to His will. We have to do it voluntarily. On the other hand, we can't fill ourselves with the Holy Spirit. *God* has to do that. But when we *do* surrender our wills fully to Him, He *will* fill us with His Spirit.

One of the great British New Testament scholars of our generation was Vincent Taylor. He declared: "Sin is self-coronation." Alongside that is what I believe to be a corollary truth: "Sanctification is self-crucifixion." Ultimately we either let self be crucified and Christ crowned as Lord of all, or, refusing to do this, self is crowned as Lord of all in our lives, and Christ is crucified afresh by our self-will.

Jesus said: "Whoever loses his life for me will find it" (Matt. 16:25). We sing: "Let me lose myself and find it Lord, in Thee." The only way we can really *find* ourselves is to *lose* ourselves in Christ.

Nowhere is the application of that truth more significantly stated than in our text for today, Gal. 2:20. The KJV states: "I am crucified with Christ: nevertheless I live; yet not I, but Christ liveth in me."

In the original Greek the first clause of this verse says: *Christo synestauromai*—"with Christ I have been crucified." The pefect tense in Greek emphasizes two things: (1) a completed act; (2) a continuing state. What the Greek says here is: "I have been, and still am, crucified with Christ."

In the KJV the second clause reads: "Nevertheless I live." But the original Greek says just the opposite: *zo de ouketi ego*—"and *no longer* do I live." *Ouketi* cannot mean "nevertheless." It means "no longer." And the *ego* (taken over into English as "ego") is emphatic: "no longer do *I* live."

The Greek text of the third clause reads: *ze de en emoi christos*—"but in me lives Christ." What Paul is saying is this: "Christ has taken the place of the carnal ego in control of my life." That is what it means to be sanctified wholly (1 Thess. 5:23). We experience both a crucifixion with Christ and also a new resurrection life in Him.

II. The Work of Faith (3:3)

In the Epistle to the Galatians Paul presents sanctification not only as the crucifixion of the carnal self (2:20) but also as the work of faith (3:3). Starting in the middle of verse 2, Paul poses critical questions: "Did you receive the Spirit by observing the law, or by believing what you heard? Are you so foolish? After beginning with the Spirit, are you now trying to attain your goal [or, reach perfection] by human effort?"

A careful reading of this Epistle will show exactly why Paul wrote it. He and Barnabas, on their first missionary journey (Acts 13—14), had founded churches in the Roman province of Galatia, which was in the center of Asia Minor (modern Turkey). Later Paul heard that some Judaizers had gone in and told the new Gentile converts that in order to be saved they had to be circumcised and keep the law of Moses.

Perhaps some of the converts protested: "Paul told us that all we had to do to be saved was to repent and believe on the Lord Jesus. We did believe, and we know we *are* saved."

I can almost hear the Judaizers say: "Yes, but if you want to be made perfect" (3:3, KJV), "you must keep all the outward ordinances of the Mosaic law."

Paul protested against this. In essence he told them: "You were justified through faith; you will be sanctified through faith. It is all of faith."

But what does faith mean?

John G. Paton was the pioneer missionary to the New Hebrides. Arriving there, he soon learned the language so that he could preach the gospel to the people.

Then he felt the need of translating the Word of God into their language, so they could read it for themselves. But he ran into a serious problem: Their language was full of *concrete* terms, but almost entirely lacking in *abstract* ones. They had words for "house," "tree," "stone," and so forth, but nothing for "love," "joy," or "peace." Worst of all he found no word suggesting the idea of believing. How can you tell people to believe in the Lord Jesus Christ when they have no word for "believe"?

One day he was sitting in his rude hut, feeling frustrated with his problem. Suddenly the door opened and an old man entered. He had walked a long distance and was tired. So he slumped down in a chair. As he did so, he said, "I'm leaning my whole weight on this chair."

Immediately the Holy Spirit said to John G. Paton, "That's it!" He turned to the man and asked, "What did you say?"

"I'm leaning my whole weight on this chair."

In the New Testament for that primitive tribe, "Believe on Jesus" became: "Lean your whole weight on Jesus." That's what faith really is!

III. The Fruit of the Spirit (5:22-23)

In the Epistle to the Galatians sanctification is presented not only as the crucifixion of the carnal self (2:20) and the work of faith (3:3) but also as the fruit of the Spirit (5:22-23).

The word *but* at the beginning of verse 22 should be heavily underscored: It points up the colossal contrast between "the works of the flesh" and "the fruit of the Spirit." Every one of the works of the flesh listed in verses 19-21 is divisive: divisive of nations, of communities, of churches, of homes, and worst of all, of hearts.

In contrast to this, every characteristic mentioned in verses 22 and 23 is a uniting element. And the greatest uniting force in all the world is love. "The fruit of the Spirit is love."

People often speak of "the fruits of the Spirit." But that is unscriptural. The Bible does not use that expression anywhere. It says, "the fruit of the Spirit."

"Yes," you say, "but these verses proceed to list nine items. How can you use the singular verb here?"

John Wesley made a helpful suggestion at this point in his *Explanatory Notes upon the New Testament,* published in 1755. He said of "love": "It is the root of all the rest."

This is logically sound. The Bible says, "God is love" (1 John 4:8, 16). It also clearly teaches that the Holy Spirit is God. So when our hearts are filled with the Holy Spirit, they are filled with love. Then this agape love will show itself in joy, peace, patience, and the other things mentioned here.

Entire sanctification means "perfect love" (1 John 4:16-18). That was John Wesley's favorite designation for this experience.

The first thing that love produces is "joy." What is joy?

Once when I was holding an evangelistic campaign in a church, I noticed a girl in the audience who never smiled. It was depressing! I couldn't get a smile out of her, no matter how hard I tried.

Years later I returned to that church. Sue was smiling all over! Eagerly I asked somebody what had happened to Sue since I was there previously. The person replied: "Oh, didn't you know? She has fallen in love with John."

If falling in love with another human being can make a person come alive like that, what ought falling in love with Jesus do to us? It should fill us with joy!

Someone has said: "Joy is the echo of God's life within us." Also: "Joy is the reflection of spiritual health in the soul." This is scriptural. We are all familiar with the Old Testament declaration: "The joy of the Lord is your strength" (Neh. 8:10). A joyful Christian is a strong Christian! And let us not forget: A joyless Christian is a weak Christian. Let's rejoice in the Lord and be strong!

The next item is "peace." The Greek word is *eirene,* from which we get "Irene." Any girl with that name should be a peaceful person!

When we are justified freely, we have peace *with* God through our Lord Jesus Christ. When we are sanctified wholly, the peace *of* God fills our souls, because the civil war inside between the old carnal nature with which we were born and the new Christ nature that came in at conversion has been ended by the full surrender of our will to God's will and the consequent crucifixion of the carnal self—as we have already noted.

Dr. J. B. Chapman once said: "Peace is the consciousness of adequate resources to meet every emergency of life."

In the depression days, my wife and I once invited another couple to eat lunch with us in a restaurant. As we were waiting for the waitress to come, I suddenly felt uneasy. Under the tablecloth I pulled out my wallet. My worst fears were confirmed: I only had a five dollar bill! Desperately I prayed: "Lord, help them to order a small hamburg sandwich!"

One day I took care of that forever: I got an American Express Card. Now I can say to guests, "Order whatever you like." That little green card will take care of even lobster tail! When we are filled with the Holy Spirit we have that peace because we know that *He* can handle any emergency that may confront us!

The next item is "patience." The Greek word is *macrothymia*, which is correctly translated "longsuffering" in the KJV.

All human beings have different personality traits: we differ in our likes and dislikes, in our tastes and preferences. So we have to be longsuffering with each other, even as sanctified Christians. But if the Holy Spirit fills our hearts with divine love, He can help us learn to practice patience with each other.

The next virtue is "kindness." In 1 Cor. 13:4 Paul also puts these two together in the same order: "Love is patient, love is kind." Instinctively we feel that kindness is one of the main manifestations of love. Let's practice it, then! Our lives should show kindness to everybody every day.

We should remember, however, that it takes time for fruit to grow. If I plant an apple tree, I don't go out the next day to pick ripe apples off it. So we should allow time for the newly sanctified to show the fruit of the Spirit growing in their lives. And we should not allow Satan to browbeat us if we are not showing the full fruit of kindness right away.

The next thing that love produces is "goodness." What is goodness?

Some people think that because they don't lie, cheat, steal, or do any "bad things" they are good. But goodness is not a negative thing; it is positive.

The best definition of goodness I have read is in Charles R. Erdman's commentary on Galatians. He says that goodness is "love in action." We are not good because of anything we don't do; we are only good as we are acting in love. That truth confronts all of us with a tremendous challenge!

The next virtue is "faithfulness." The Greek word *pistis* means both "faith" and "faithfulness." But the context clearly shows that here the latter is meant, as all new versions have.

Paul goes on to say that love shows itself in "gentleness." The main symbol of the Holy Spirit in the Bible is the gentle dove. That is shown by the fact that in all three Synoptic Gospels we are told that at Jesus' baptism the Holy Spirit came down on Him as a dove (Matt. 3:16; Mark 1:10; Luke 3:22).

In the Song of Songs we find doves mentioned many times. In one passage (1:15), the Lover says to his Beloved:

"How beautiful you are, my darling!
Oh, how beautiful!
Your eyes are doves."

Unfortunately, some professing Christians do not have eyes like a dove; they have hawk's eyes!

We have seen a hawk soaring very high in the sky. Suddenly it took a power dive, grabbed a chicken or field mouse in its beak, and flew off to devour it. We wondered how the hawk could spot that tiny object so far away, and we were told that hawk's eyes have telescopic lens.

If we are proud that we can spot the least little fault in others, let's ask God to take off those telescopic lens and install wide-angle lens, so we can see life and see it whole. Perhaps if we had the background of that person we criticize, we would be worse than he is!

The last virtue mentioned is "self-control." This is more than "temperance" (KJV). It is a matter of keeping our whole life—our actions, words, and attitudes—under control by the help of the Spirit.

Conclusion:

Rees Howells was converted in the United States about the time of the great Welsh Revival. Returning to Wales, he soon started out preaching the gospel in villages around him, and God gave him souls.

But one day the Holy Spirit began to deal with him definitely about a deeper need of his heart. He describes it this way:

36

It was unconditional surrender. . . . It took five days to make the decision. Like Isaiah, I saw the holiness of God, and seeing Him, I saw my own corrupt nature. . . . I knew I had to be cleansed.

He continues: "First there was the love of money." Finally came the fifth day of his dying out to himself. The Holy Spirit asked him: "Now, are you willing?"

Rees Howells wanted to say yes, but he found himself unable to do so. Again the Spirit spoke: "I have been dealing with you for five days; you must give me your decision by six o'clock tonight."

Rees Howells writes: "I asked Him for more time, but He said, 'You will not have a minute after six o'clock.'"

Once more the Spirit asked, "Are you willing?"

Rees Howells tells us: "It was ten minutes to six. . . . Five to six came. I could count the ticks of the clock."

Finally came the climax. He records:

> Then the Spirit spoke again: "If you can't be willing, would you like me to help you? Are you willing to be made willing?". . . . It was one minute to six. I bowed my head and said, "Lord, I am willing." . . . Within an hour the Third Person of the Godhead had come in. (*Rees Howells, Intercessor,* 43)

What is the price we pay to receive this experience? We have to die out to self, surrender our will fully to God's will.

The songwriter put it well:

> *All to Jesus I surrender.*
> *Make me, Saviour, wholly thine;*
> *Let me feel the Holy Spirit,*
> *Truly know that Thou art mine.*

The chorus:

> *I surrender all. I surrender all.*
> *All to Thee, my blessed Saviour, I surrender all.*

Will you make that your prayer? Right now?

6

EPHESIANS
The Holy Church

Scripture: Eph. 1:3, 13-14; 4:30; 5:25-33
Text: Eph. 5:25-27

Introduction:

We are faced with a real challenge in three outstanding expressions in the first chapter of Ephesians.

The first one is in the third verse. In the KJV it is translated "in heavenly places," in the NIV "in the heavenly realms." The Greek has simply: *en tois epouraniois*—literally, "in the heavenlies." It occurs five times in this Epistle and is really the keynote of Ephesians, which presents life in the heavenlies. It is in *heavenly fellowship* with Christ that we experience "every spiritual blessing" (singular in the Greek), as verse 3 tells us, "Fellowship divine! Oh, what blessed, sweet communion!"

The second expression is in verse 13. It is the verb *sealed* (KJV). When we speak now of "sealing" a letter we mean licking the glue and fastening the flap on the envelope. The Greek verb *sphragizo* means to "stamp with a seal." The NIV says: "you were marked in him [Christ] with a seal."

Archaeologists have dug up many cylindrical seals from the Babylonian and Persian periods. A servant would take a piece of soft clay and mold it into a cylinder about the size of the human thumb. On this round clay cylinder he would inscribe the insignia of his master. Then he would bake it hard in a kiln.

When the master wanted to send a bale of goods down the Euphrates River, the servant would put soft wax where the bundle was tied together. Then on this soft wax he would make a complete rotation of the cylindrical seal, leaving an oblong imprint of the master's insignia. This would show that the bundle belonged to this particular man.

In the period when Paul wrote, the seal was a signet ring worn by every wealthy Roman. He would stamp the wax with his ring.

The point is this: No man had a right to place his seal on anything unless it was really his property. Just so, God cannot stamp us with His seal, the Holy Spirit, until we give ourselves wholly to Him. When we surrender our will completely to His will, to be His—body, soul, and spirit, for time and eternity—then God will mark us in Christ with a seal, the promised Holy Spirit.

Our third expression is in verse 14. The Greek word is *arrabon* (KJV, "earnest").

The earliest meaning of this, found in classical Greek, is "a down payment guaranteeing that the rest will be paid." So we read that the Holy Spirit is "a deposit guaranteeing our inheritance" (NIV). The Holy Spirit is the down payment on our heavenly home. What will heaven be like? It will be like those times when the Holy Spirit makes the presence of Jesus most real to our hearts. That is a foretaste of heaven.

The word *arrabon* (in the form *arrabona*) has a very striking use in modern Greek, where it means "an engagement ring." This is a very beautiful thought. When we are converted, there begins a loving courtship with Christ. But finally He asks, "Will you be Mine, only Mine, forever Mine?" If we say a full yes to that, He slips the engagement ring on our finger, the Holy Spirit in our heart.

It is important that we keep this heavenly engagement ring. Eph. 4:30 urges: "And do not grieve the Holy Spirit of God, with whom you were sealed for the day of redemption."

How may we grieve the Holy Spirit? Certainly by deliberate disobedience. But we can also grieve Him by ignoring Him, making Him the unwelcome guest in our hearts. Unwelcome guests usually leave!

Now to consider our text—Eph. 5:25-27. Verse 25 points out *the provision for our sanctification in the death of Christ,* in verse 26 *the prerequisite of our sanctification in the washing of regeneration,* and in verse 27 *the purpose of our sanctification in our presentation to Christ as His bride.*

I. The Provision for Our Sanctification in the Death of Christ

The Golden Text of the Bible is John 3:16: "For God so loved the world that he gave his one and only Son, that whoever believes in him shall not perish but have eternal life." Now, in Eph. 5:25-26 we find: "Husbands, love your wives, just as Christ loved the church and gave himself up for her to make her holy."

Heb. 13:12 corroborates this. It says: "And so Jesus also suffered outside the city gate to make the people holy [or, sanctify the people] through his own blood." When we realize that Christ suffered on the Cross not only to save us but also to sanctify us, it should warn us of the terrible ingratitude we show when we do not go on and get sanctified wholly. We should not let His sufferings for our sanctification be in vain!

40

II. The Prerequisite of Our Sanctification in the Washing of Regeneration

We go on now to verse 26: That he might *"make her holy* [sanctify her], cleansing her by the washing with water through the word" (NIV) or, "the washing of regeneration" (Titus 3:5, KJV).

"Cleansing" here is the aorist participle *catherisas.* Greek grammars agree that the aorist participle normally indicates action antecedent to the main verb. So the correct translation is: "having cleansed." What the Greek says is that Christ, having cleansed the church in the washing of regeneration, purposes to sanctify her. And "sanctify" here is in the aorist subjunctive, suggesting a crisis experience rather than a long, drawn-out process.

Incidentally, the Greek word for "church," *ecclesia* (v. 25), is feminine, and all the pronouns that refer back to it are feminine in Greek. Furthermore, the picture here is of the church as the bride of Christ (see vv. 31-32). And since a bride is not an "it" (KJV), the word is "her" (NIV).

And now to the third point, in verse 27:

III. The Purpose of Our Sanctification in Our Presentation to Christ as His Bride

Why did Christ die on the Cross? In order that having cleansed His Church with the washing of regeneration, and sanctified her, He might "present her to himself as a radiant church, without stain or wrinkle or any other blemish, but holy and blameless."

The expression "without stain or wrinkle" suggests to us the idea of being "washed and ironed." Let's pursue that idea.

I have watched my wife turn on the hot water in the washing machine and put detergent in it. Then she puts in some soiled clothes. I can almost hear them groaning as they are shoved down in that hot, sudsy water. Then she pushes a button and the agitator pushes those clothes around. By now I can almost hear them groaning out loud.

Then comes the second stage. Before we had electric dryers, there was a wringer on the top of the washing machine. I liked to tuck a corner of the mouth of a pillow slip in between the rollers. As the rollers kept turning, the mouth of that pillow slip would finally be closed. Some people I knew never did go through God's wringer because they never got their big mouths shut!

Still the rollers would turn relentlessly. The pillow slip would fight back, puffing up more and more. But finally it would come out flat. And I know again that some people have never gone through God's wringer because they never got their puff and pride squeezed out of them.

But one stage was still left—the ironing board. For Jesus wants His bride to be "without stain or wrinkle." And when we meet Him as our heavenly Bridegroom at the "wedding supper of the Lamb" (Rev. 19:9), we want to be sure that we are "without stain or wrinkle" as we are presented to Him. So let's get the wrinkles out of our personalities by submitting to the Holy Spirit's ironing process. It doesn't feel comfortable, but it's important. And that ironing process goes on throughout our lives down here.

Many years ago I heard a man give a striking testimony at a camp meeting. He had been a civil engineer commissioned by our government to plot the path of the Pan American highway through Central America.

After many days of hard work in the hot sun, he received a telegram from Washington asking him to come back immediately. So he hastened down to the harbor city to catch a plane back to the States. He went to sleep, dreaming of a nice cool flight back home.

But that night God called him on the heavenly phone. "Where are you going tomorrow?"

"I'm going back to Washington."

Then the Lord said, "I have another errand for you to take care of first. You remember that new convert Pedro up in the mountains? He is walking in all the light he has, but his heart is hungry for a deeper experience. I want you to go back and tell him how to be sanctified wholly."

"But Lord, my boss told me to come back to Washington immediately."

The Lord answered him, "Who is your boss, anyway?"

This man was sanctified wholly, and so he promptly replied, "You are, Lord. But I was told that they had some great project waiting for me, like plotting another Panama or Suez Canal."

I shall never forget what the man next related in his testimony. Looking very serious, he told us: "The Lord said to me, 'I'm a lot more interested in Pedro being sanctified wholly than I am in your becoming a great, world-renowned engineer.'"

We need to get God's perspective on life. He puts the highest premium on our having a clean heart and living a holy life. Have *you* been sanctified wholly? If not, make this your prayer:

> *Lord Jesus, I long to be perfectly whole;*
> *I want Thee forever to live in my soul.*
> *Break down every idol, cast out every foe.*
> *Now wash me and I shall be whiter than snow.*

"Whiter than snow" means that we have been inwardly cleansed from the sinful nature. We are clean through and through.

7

1 THESSALONIANS
Sanctification: The Will of God

Scripture: 1 Thess. 1:4-10; 3:12—4:7; 5:23-24

Text: 1 Thess. 4:3—"It is God's will that you should be sanctified."

Introduction:

Two important questions are often asked of us who are of the Wesleyan persuasion. The first is: "Where do you get the term *entire sanctification?*"

The answer is found clearly in 1 Thess. 5:23. The KJV states it: "And the very God of peace sanctify you wholly." This means entire sanctification. In fact, the *New American Standard Bible* has "sanctify you entirely."

The Greek adverb is *holoteleis,* found only here in the New Testament. It is a strong compound, composed of *holos* —"whole, complete, entire"—and *telos,* "end." So it literally means "wholly-completely" or "completely-entirely."

In his famous German New Testament, made in 1522, Martin Luther translated this compound as *durch und durch,* "through and through." I suggested to our Committee on Bible Translation that we adopt this English rendering for the

NIV, and it was done. Later I discovered that the Arndt and Gingrich *Greek-English Lexicon of the New Testament* suggested "through and through" for this passage. So the New Testament does teach entire sanctification as a complete cleansing from all sin.

The second question is: "Why do you say that this is a second crisis in Christian experience, after conversion?"

To find the answer to this question we must turn back to the first chapter. There in verse 9 Paul is addressing those who "turned to God from idols to serve the living and true God." In other words, the readers of this Epistle were born-again Christians who had forsaken their pagan background to serve the Lord.

Also in verse 7 Paul writes: "And so you became a model to all the believers in Macedonia and Achaia." These new converts were living exemplary Christian lives. They were not backslidden; they were even *model* Christians.

In the third place, the apostle says in verse 8: "The Lord's message rang out from you not only in Macedonia and Achaia—your faith in God has become known everywhere." Here were people who were genuinely converted, living exemplary lives, and propagating the good news of salvation. And yet Paul wrote to them: "It is God's will that *you* should be sanctified" (4:3). Entire sanctification is not something for sinners, but only for believers. It is definitely a "second work of grace."

There are three things to consider in connection with the meaning of entire sanctification. It means: (1) Purity; (2) Power; and (3) Perfect Love.

I. Purity

Under the general heading of "purity" first think of "purity of life."

There once was a party of tourists visiting a coal mine. Before they descended to the tunnel below, the old guide who was assigned to them brought out some coveralls and suggested they put them on to protect their clothes from the coal dust in the mine.

In the group was a girl who was wearing a pretty white dress. (This must have been a long time ago!) She didn't want to put on those ugly coveralls, and so protested. When the guide rather insisted, she got a bit uppish and said, "I guess I can go down into that coal mine with this white dress on, if I want to."

The old man looked at her a moment in silence and then gently replied: "Yes, you can go down into the mine with that white dress, but you can't come back out of the coal mine with a white dress on."

I have had many young people say to me, "Can't I be a Christian and go here or there, or do this or that?" That is a completely wrong question to ask. What we should be asking is: "Can I do this or that, go to this place or the other, and come back as good a Christian as I was before?" That is the *real* question.

I also heard of a man who, one morning, was dressing to go to his office. Meanwhile, his wife was dutifully getting breakfast in the kitchen.

Suddenly he called from the bedroom: "Martha, Martha, come here quick and tell me whether this shirt's clean enough to wear another day."

Wisely, Martha didn't leave the porridge to burn over on the stove. Instead she called back: "No, Henry, there's no need for me to come in and look at that shirt. If it's doubtful, it's dirty." And I submit to you that if a man thought it was doubtful, it surely was dirty!

From this incident I have deduced this important motto: "If in doubt, *don't!*" There are plenty of undoubtedly good things to take up all our time and attention every day without our fooling around with anything that is at all doubtful.

In 1 Thess. 4:7 Paul writes: "For God did not call us to be impure, but to live a holy life." A holy life is a clean life, a godly life. In this day of careless, and even promiscuous, living, we must be careful to live according to God's standards, as set out in His Word.

Sanctification means not only purity of life but also purity of heart. Let us look again at 1 Thess. 5:23. God wants to sanctify us "through and through," cleansing our hearts from all sin and filling them with His Holy Spirit. Furthermore, the verb *sanctify* here is in the aorist tense, which suggests a momentary act. We are to have a crisis experience of complete cleansing.

Cleansing from what? Many of us have heard most of our lives that we are to be cleansed from the carnal nature. But what is carnality?

I once heard a preacher say that he saw a woman get a little tense one day. She excused herself by saying, "It's my nerves." The preacher exclaimed: "Nerves—nonsense! It's sheer carnality!"

I'd like to tie that preacher into a kitchen for a few hours. He's trying to cook something on the stove. A little two-year-old daughter is tugging at his clothes and whining that she doesn't feel good. About that time the baby wakes up in the bedroom and begins to scream his head off. He starts for the bedroom, only to be interrupted by the front doorbell ringing. As he heads for that, the telephone buzzes loudly. I'd like to see then if he had any nerves!

The truth is that nerves are a part of our physical body. We all have them. But we *do* need to learn to control them by the help of the indwelling Holy Spirit. That is a part of growth in grace, after we are sanctified.

In our first pastorate we had an evangelist who asserted emphatically from the pulpit: "All impatience is carnality!" Where do we draw the line between patience and impatience? All of us are relatively patient and yet sometimes feel a bit impatient to get moving. No; impatience, in and of itself, is not carnality.

"Oh," you say, "I know what carnality is; it's anger." Well, if that be true, then Jesus was carnal. In Mark 3:5 we read that Jesus "looked around at them in anger," being "deeply distressed at their stubborn hearts." The Pharisees didn't want Jesus to heal the man with the withered hand because it was the Sabbath day; let the man suffer another 24 hours.

The verb *looked around* is *periblepsamenos,* an aorist participle including a momentary flash of anger at the cruel, selfish attitude of these religious leaders. But "deeply distressed"—or "being grieved" (KJV)—is the present tense of continuous attitude. We are immediately to abhor sin but always to love the sinner.

What, then, is carnality, or "the sinful nature" as we call it in the NIV? It is self-will, wishing to have our own way rather than God's way. That is what God wants to cleanse from our hearts in the experience of entire sanctification.

We need not only purity of life and purity of heart but also purity of mind. In entire sanctification "the body of sin" (Rom. 6:6) is "destroyed" (KJV) or "done away with" (NIV). But though this happens to the sinful nature, our human nature still remains. Holiness does not dehumanize us.

Some people say, "It doesn't matter what I look at or listen to; my heart is pure." I don't buy that! I don't believe that young people can sit and look at everything on television for hours at a time without its affecting their spiritual experience. We can't fill our mind with filth without some of it filtering down into our heart. Let's be careful what we look at, and guard our thoughts carefully.

II. Power

Sanctification is not only purity but power. The word *power* occurs only once in 1 Thessalonians, in 1:5. Paul writes: "Our gospel came to you not simply with words, but also with power, with the Holy Spirit"—that is, with the power of the Holy Spirit. Jesus said to His disciples: "You will receive power when the Holy Spirit comes on you" (Acts 1:8).

The Greek word for "power" is *dynamis,* from which we get three English words: *dynamite, dynamo,* and *dynamic.* These suggest that the Holy Spirit gives us explosive power to overcome all obstacles, electric power being generated in our hearts and lives every day, and excelling power to live dynamic lives and to make us soul winners.

Some time ago I read of a wealthy American who bought a Rolls Royce. He was delighted with its seemingly unlimited power. But, like most men, he wanted to know how many horsepower it had.

The dealer said, "I don't know." When the owner insisted that he find out, the dealer wrote to the company in England. Finally he called the owner and told him that he had received a reply. "How many horsepower?" asked the man. The dealer answered: "I received a telegram of just one word: 'Adequate.'" That is what the Holy Spirit gives us: adequate power to meet every emergency in life!

III. Perfect Love

The third thing that sanctification means is perfect love, as described clearly in 1 John 4:16-18. Here in 1 Thess. 3:12-13 we read about this love that fills our hearts and overflows to others.

The Greek language has three words for love. The lowest term is *eros,* which we have taken over into English in the adjective *erotic.* As this suggests, the word *eros* had bad connotations. It is never used in the New Testament. I call it "Hollywood love."

The second word is *philia.* It occurs only once in the New Testament, in James 4:4 where it is translated "friendship." The related verb *phileo* is translated "kiss" as well as "love."

So *philia* is friendship love, affectionate love. I call it "homey love."

But the dominant word for love in the New Testament is *agape*, which means unselfish love that seeks the highest good of its object. That is the word here. It means "holy love." Paul prayed that the love of the Thessalonian Christians might overflow. Only that which is full can overflow.

Dr. Nathan Wood was president of Gordon Divinity School. Both Mrs. Earle and I took a course in theology under him. We agreed that if we ever saw a person who was filled with the Holy Spirit, Dr. Wood was that.

One day, after teaching morning classes at Eastern Nazarene College, I went into Boston for an afternoon class at Gordon. When I arrived, the place seemed deserted. Puzzled, I looked around and soon discovered the faculty and students gathered in chapel for an all day of prayer.

Quietly entering, I heard one student after another stand up and pray out loud. Two petitions I heard particularly impressed me. A student would pray, "Lord, cleanse my heart from all sin." Then another would pray, "O Lord, fill me with Your Holy Spirit."

When the meeting broke up, I asked Dr. Wood if I could talk with him in his office. I shared my concern about the students' petitions in chapel. When they drew near to the Lord in an all day of prayer, their hearts cried out to be cleansed. But in class I heard professors say that we can't be cleansed from all sin until the time of our physical death. I then mentioned the student's petition to be filled with the Spirit. But we were told in class that we were filled with the Spirit at the time of our conversion. I also remarked that I didn't hear much at Gordon about the Holy Spirit.

To my surprise, instead of arguing with me, Dr. Wood nodded his head in agreement. "I'm afraid our younger professors don't know much about the Holy Spirit," he said. Then he related to me this incident.

He was sitting on the platform during the commencement exercises at his alma mater, Wheaton College, waiting for the honorary D.D. degree to be conferred on him. As the exercises were going on, he felt a cry rising in his heart: "O Lord, I'm not fit to be called a doctor of divinity." Of course, "Divinity" here is to be taken in the objective sense of theology. But it was typical of this man that he thought of it in the subjective sense of divine nature.

Dr. Wood told me that he finally became oblivious to all that was going on around him. Desperately he was crying out in his soul: "O Lord, fix me up inside so I'll be fit to be called a doctor of divinity!"

Just then he heard his name called. He stood to his feet and listened as the citation was read. Then he stepped forward. He told me this: "As the president and the dean draped the doctor's hood down over my head and on to my shoulders, I felt something like an electric shock go through me, from the top of my head to the tip of my toes, and I received a mighty baptism of the Holy Spirit." No wonder we sensed that he was a Spirit-filled man! He was asked to go throughout New England speaking in Baptist churches on the Holy Spirit. He said that people were eager to hear about his experience at Wheaton.

Let us pray this prayer:

> *Have Thine own way, Lord!*
> *Have thine own way!*
> *Hold o'er my being*
> *Absolute sway!*
> *Fill with Thy Spirit*
> *Till all shall see*
> *Christ only, always,*
> *Living in me!*

8

HEBREWS

The Perseverance of the Saints

Scripture: Heb. 12:1-3, 14
Text: Heb. 12:14

Introduction:

Nineteen hundred fifty-four was a great year in the world of athletics. For the first time in recorded history the mile was officially run in less than four minutes. And two men did it that year.

On May 6, Roger Bannister, a 25-year-old English medical student ran a mile in 3 minutes, 59.4 seconds.

On June 21, John Landy, a 24-year-old Australian, ran it in 3 minutes, 58 seconds.

On August 7 these two 4-minute milers competed together, for the first time, in the British games at Vancouver, B.C., in the so-called Miracle Mile. There were many other competitors that day. But instinctively all the spectators knew that either Bannister or Landy would win.

Sure enough, when the pistol cracked, these two men were soon out in front of all the rest. Landy led until the last

100 yards. Then he became obsessed with the question: "Where's Roger?"

Finally, he couldn't stand it any longer, and he looked over his shoulder. And there was Roger, right behind him. But as Landy turned to look, he fumbled a step, and Bannister surged past him to win the race in 3 minutes, 58.8 seconds. Landy came in a poor second at 3 minutes, 59.6 seconds. He lost the race by eight-tenths of a second! What could possibly be more frustrating?

But here's the point. *Time* magazine recorded in 1954 that Landy said to newspaper reporters: "If I hadn't turned to look at Roger, I would have won."

This brings us to our Scripture lesson at the beginning of the 12th chapter of Hebrews, verse 1: "Therefore, since we are surrounded by such a great cloud of witnesses, let us throw off everything that hinders and the sin that so easily entangles, and let us run with perseverance the race marked out for us."

The first word, "Therefore," always points back to what immediately precedes. And what is that here? It is the great "faith chapter" of the Bible: Hebrews 11. There are the names of many of the Old Testament heroes of faith. They are filling the grandstands, as it were, and cheering us on. We can almost hear them shouting: "We made it through to the end, and you can too!"

The author of Hebrews then gives a fourfold exhortation. First he urges us: "Let us throw off everything that hinders."

We never did see anyone winning a race while wearing hip boots and a heavy overcoat—not unless it was a handicap race. From ancient Greek runners in the famous Marathon races, participants have always stripped down to the barest necessities. And we must "throw off" all worldly baggage if we are going to run the Christian race successfully. All hindrances must be discarded immediately.

For the second exhortation, the writer adds: "and the sin that so easily entangles." The KJV says: "and the sin which doth so easily beset us." Thus, people think it means some "besetting sin" they are guilty of. The Greek literally says: "and the sin that clings so closely to us." Twice in the seventh chapter of Romans Paul uses the expression: "sin living in me" (vv. 17, 20). He also calls it: "the law of sin at work within my members" (v. 23). In Rom. 8:7 he refers to it as "the carnal mind" (KJV) or "the sinful mind" (NIV). In many circles it has commonly been called "the carnal nature." It is the greatest single hindrance to our running the Christian race. We need to have our hearts cleansed from "all sin" (1 John 1:7), if we are going to be free to run with full strength. Sin weakens us.

The third exhortation is: "Let us run with perseverance the race marked out for us." The KJV says, "with patience." But it takes more than patience to win a race; it takes *perseverance!* The Greek word literally means "endurance." That is what it takes to win a long-distance race. And the Christian race lasts all the rest of our lives. So we must have "perseverance."

The fourth exhortation is found in verse 2. Now we come to the application of our opening illustration, for it says: "Let us fix our eyes on Jesus." If we look around at others, we are going to fumble and falter and fail as Landy did. Jesus is waiting at the end of the race to welcome us as victors (2 Tim. 4:6-8). If we keep our eyes on him, we will make it.

It is obvious that the picture portrayed in these opening verses of the 12th chapter of Hebrews is that of a long-distance (Marathon) race. But too few people have realized that this metaphor carries over to our text, verse 14.

The KJV says, "Follow peace." But the Greek verb is *dioko,* which means "pursue" (NASB). And it is in the present imperative of continuous action: "Keep on pursuing."

This verb *dioko* was used in classical Greek for an animal pursuing its prey. We might illustrate this.

Some years ago I was preaching at a church in Missouri. We were invited out to a farm home for Sunday dinner. While the meal was being prepared, I sauntered down by the barn.

Soon the pastor and the man of the place came down and joined me. The latter showed me his thoroughbred hunting hounds and then related to me what I want to share with you.

He said that sometimes on Saturday morning he would set his dogs loose. Barking excitedly, they would race out to the open field and woods.

After awhile their barking turned to baying, and he knew they were on the trail of a fox. Then the fox would lead them for a merry chase. He would circle back across his trail, and that would confuse them. He would cross a shallow creek, causing them to bark loudly as they lost the trail for a little while. The owner said to me: "I have actually sat down to milk my cow at five o'clock in the afternoon, and I would still hear those dogs baying on the track of that 'foxy' fox."

If we would pursue peace and holiness as persistently and perseveringly as a common hound dog, we would all succeed. What we need is *dogged* perseverance!

Our text suggests four propositions.

I. You can't pursue peace with people successfully unless you first make peace with God. Probably no thoughtful Christian would question that.

II. You can't *maintain* peace with God unless you *keep on* pursuing peace with people. The vertical relationship is primary. But the horizontal relationship is also essential.

The story is told of a couple sitting together on the buckboard seat of a farm wagon, as they drove along a country road. In front of them were two horses prancing along in perfect step on either side of the wagon tongue.

It so happened that things hadn't been going too well at home. Mary became rather pensive and sad. Finally she turned to her husband and said, "John, wouldn't it be wonderful if we could go through life together in perfect step, like those two horses."

John took one look at the horses and then growled out of the corner of his mouth: "We could if we had only one tongue between us like they have!"

Of course, the $64.00 question is: "Whose tongue is it going to be, his or hers?" And the answer is: "Both tongues must be on the altar, subservient to God's will and governed by divine love."

III. The third proposition is: You can't pursue holiness without getting sanctified wholly. We have known many individuals who, without any Wesleyan teaching, have been cleansed from all sin and filled with the Holy Spirit simply because they earnestly sought God's will with all their heart. Jesus said:

> "Blessed are those who hunger and thirst for
> righteousness, for they will be filled."

Paul declared: "It is God's will that you should be sanctified" (1 Thess. 4:3). In the same Epistle he defines what that sanctification is by praying that God "may sanctify you entirely" (NASB), "wholly" (KJV), or "through and through" (NIV). Entire sanctification is God's will for all His people.

Now we come to the fourth proposition:

IV. You can't keep sanctified without pursuing holiness all our life.

In effect the text says: "Keep on pursuing peace with all people, and keep on pursuing holiness of heart and life; if you don't, you will never see the Lord." If we want to spend a happy eternity in the light of His glorious presence, that is what we all must do. It is a lifelong pursuit. Failure to follow this pursuit can bring tragic results, here and hereafter.

Some years ago a pastor's wife in Florida shared with me a very moving experience. One day she held a service for women in a jail in the city where her husband pastored. At the close of her message, with everyone's eyes closed, she asked anyone who felt the need of prayer to lift her hand. A girl sitting in the back seat did so.

After the service was dismissed, the speaker made her way back to this girl. Taking her by the hand, she looked down into the face of a naturally rather pretty teenager and said: "Honey, you don't look like a girl who belongs in here."

Tears filled the girl's eyes, and she said: "No, I wasn't made for a place like this. You see, I've lived all my life in a Nazarene parsonage." When the pastor's wife asked what had happened, the girl shared this story with her.

She had lived a good life in high school but had never been sanctified wholly. One Sunday night her father preached a strong sermon on holiness and gave an invitation for seekers.

A lady stepped across the aisle and asked the girl if she would like to go to the altar and pray. The girl shook her head and said, "No, I'm all right." But the Holy Spirit was convicting her of her need.

Finally the girl turned around and left the church. She said that as she walked out the door she felt an awful sense that she wanted to have her fling. When we close the door of our heart to God we open it to Satan, and he will do his worst.

Later, she took up with a worthless girl in town. This one suggested, "Let's go to Florida!" And so they started out.

It wasn't long until they ran out of money and began thumbing for a ride. That night a man came along, stopped, and invited them to get in. They climbed into the front seat with him, our girl sitting next to the driver.

She said that as they rode on through the hours of the night they stopped at almost every tavern and went in for a drink. This girl, who was brought up in a Christian home and had never touched a drop of liquor, was drinking that night with a godless stranger. When we deliberately walk away from God we put ourselves on the devil's toboggan slide, and never dream how *fast* and how *far* we may go down the hill to our ruin!

In the early hours of the morning the man said to the girls, "Do you have any money?" They replied, "No; that's why we were hitchhiking."

The man cried out, "I've got to have a drink. If I don't, I'll die." What a pity!

Just then they saw a car parked beside the road. Its driver had become sleepy, so he had pulled over to the side, turned off the motor, and stretched out on the front seat—without locking the car doors!

The man with whom the girls were riding pulled over, yanked the other car door open, and demanded the billfold of the now wide-awake traveler. Instead of complying, the man jumped out of the car and started wrestling with his would-be robber. When the first man saw that he was getting the worst of the struggle, he stabbed the resisting man in the chest. Then he returned to his own car where the girls were waiting, and slumped over the steering wheel in a drunken stupor.

Soon a state patrolman came along, saw the bleeding body beside the road, stopped, and began to administer first aid. On his radio he called for an ambulance.

By this time the drunken driver was awakened by sirens blasting and bright lights shining. Glancing down, he saw the bloody knife in his hand. He slipped it to the girl beside him, saying: "Here, get this out of sight." She quickly hid it inside her dress.

When the victim was taken away in the ambulance, the police turned their attention to the other car still parked by the highway. They took the three passengers into the police station. There the bloody knife was found in the possession of the pastor's daughter. She was given a five-year sentence. Fortunately the victim lived. If he had died, she would have received life imprisonment.

The lady who related this told me: "The other day I visited the state penitentiary. The girl said to me: 'God has forgiven me and taken me back. I have gone on and gotten sanctified wholly.' Then with a wail in her voice she cried, 'But that doesn't keep me from having to spend five years behind the bars just for having my own way for a few hours.'"

Let me say to all who read this; you can't afford to have your own way. It costs too much. When the Lord asks you to surrender your will wholly to His will, say "Yes, Lord" and do it. You will never be sorry you did!

9

1 PETER

What Is a Holy Person?

Text: 1 Pet. 1:15-16

Introduction:

How does one become a holy person? Dr. A. B. Simpson, the founder of the Christian and Missionary Alliance, was one of the holiest men of his generation. How did it happen? He describes his crisis experience this way:

"The Lord Jesus revealed himself as a living and all-sufficient presence, and I learned for the first time that Christ had not saved us from future peril and left us to fight the battle of life as best we could; but He who had justified us was waiting to sanctify us, to enter into our spirit and substitute His strength, His holiness, His joy, His love, His faith, His power, for all our worthlessness, helplessness, and nothingness, and make it an actual living fact."

And Charles H. Spurgeon, one of Britain's greatest preachers and soul winners, once declared: "If I have won men to Christ, it has been because I have received the Holy Spirit."

We cannot be holy people until we have been filled with the Holy Spirit. It is His cleansing, sanctifying presence that makes us holy.

The Greek adjective *hagios,* "holy," occurs about 230 times in the New Testament. In the Septuagint, the Greek translation of the Old Testament made about 200 years before Christ, it is found nearly 500 times. This makes over 700 times that this word *holy* occurs in our Holy Bible.

In the New Testament this adjective is translated *holy* 161 times in the KJV. But also note that the word *saints* (61 times) is a translation of this same adjective in the plural. So "saints" are literally "holy ones." A holy God must have a holy people. A person is not a true saint unless he is a holy person.

The frequency of the word *holy* shows that holiness is a dominant theme in the Bible. In the Old Testament the term is applied largely to things, especially in the Pentateuch. The ancient Tabernacle had a holy place and a holy of holies, or most holy place, where God's presence dwelt. But in the New Testament it is primarily persons who are holy.

In response to the question "What Is a Holy Person?" three answers are considered.

I. A Holy Person Is One Who Is Set Apart to God

The verb *hagiazo,* "sanctify," is formed from the adjective *hagios,* "holy," and the letter *zeta,* which carries the causative effect. So it literally means "make holy." But it is generally recognized that often in the Old Testament the term *sanctify* has its minimal meaning of "set apart to God for sacred use."

If we are going to be holy people, the first thing we must do is to give ourselves completely to God—body, soul, and spirit. Unless we belong fully to Him, we are not really holy persons. And this is *our* decision; God cannot make it for us. We have to die to *self* in order to become fully alive to *God.* As long as we want to have our own way and do our own thing we cannot be holy persons. But if we are willing to consecrate ourselves completely to God, then He will sanctify us wholly, stamping us with the seal of His Holy Spirit, showing that we are now His property, belonging fully to Him.

This leads to the second answer in response to the question. It is this:

II. A Holy Person Is One Who Is Filled with the Spirit

It is only the indwelling presence of the Holy Spirit that can make *us* truly holy. We have to be emptied of self in order to be filled with himself.

This means first of all a crisis experience, as it was for the 120 disciples on the Day of Pentecost. They had tarried for about 10 days in the Upper Room, "joined together constantly in prayer" (Acts 1:14). They waited before the Lord, dying out to self, and consecrating their all to God. Finally they received the fiery baptism with the Holy Spirit, which Jesus had predicted in Acts 1:5. John the Baptist had foretold this when he said to his followers: "I baptize you with water for repentance. But after me will come one who is more powerful than I . . . He will baptize you with the Holy Spirit and with fire" (Matt. 3:11). This means a fiery baptism that would cleanse their hearts from all sin.

That is the *crisis.* But there must also be a *continuation.* In Eph. 5:18 Paul admonished his readers: "Be filled with the Spirit." Here the Greek verb is in the present tense of continuous action. So it literally means "Be continually filled with the Spirit." Only the Holy Spirit can *make* us holy and only He can *keep* us holy. It is His active, sanctifying presence in our hearts every day that enables us to be holy.

Now we come to the third answer:

III. A Holy Person Is One Who Is Living a Holy Life

Our text says: "Be holy in all you do." The KJV reads: "Be ye holy in all manner of conversation." It is true that in 1611 *conversation,* from the Latin, meant "manner of living." But it is now used in the narrower sense of "talking." The Greek word that Paul used here takes in all of life. Peter told his readers to be "holy in all you do." We are to be holy in every area of our lives. "All you do" takes in not only our words but also our attitudes and actions. We are to live holy lives every day in every way.

The basic meaning of holiness is purity. A holy life is a pure life. That means that no hint of immorality is to be tolerated in the Christian's life. In a world that is now flooded with pornography, we must be very careful what we look at and listen to. Holy people cannot be too careful at this point. We are all human, and we live in bodies that still have their physical, God-given appetites. So we must guard our lives every day against evil influences around us, and we must keep our thoughts pure.

A further word needs to be said at this point. A favorite trick of the devil is to sit on one shoulder and whisper an unclean thought into our minds—then slip around to the other shoulder and accusingly say: "See, you are not sanctified! If you were, you wouldn't have had such a thought!"

We might also describe it another way. In a world such as we live in today it is almost impossible never to have a momentary thought that we regret. But thoughts of evil are not necessarily evil thoughts. They are not that unless and until we entertain them and begin to enjoy them. It has well been said: "You can't keep birds from flying over your head, but you can keep them from building nests in your hair." It's when we *harbor* bad thoughts that we get into serious trouble.

This leads to the idea that "bad thoughts" may not necessarily be related to what we think of as immoral. In God's sight unkind, unloving thoughts are *bad* thoughts. We must not entertain them, but rather we should quickly expel them, before they affect our attitudes and perhaps our words.

A new area now opens up to us for answering the question: "What is a holy person?" It is simply this: A holy person is a loving person. Holiness means godliness, or godlikeness. And the Bible declares: "God is love" (1 John 4:8, 16). If we are not loving, we are not godly, and so we are not holy.

This is a very important point. If our hearts are filled with the Holy Spirit, they are filled with love. And we must be sure that this love is dominating our lives—not only our outward actions but also our inner attitudes and thoughts. The only way to live a holy life is to ask God to help us show a loving attitude at all times. No matter what anyone does or says *to* us, or *about* us, we must love that person and *pray* for that one. In this way we keep our hearts pure and holy, regardless of what others do.

In conclusion I should like to give my own personal testimony. I was brought up in a very godly Quaker home. We had family worship twice a day and went to church—in horse and carriage seven miles each way—every Sunday morning and evening, as well as to midweek prayer meeting. And this in spite of the fact that on our dairy farm the cows had to be milked between five and six o'clock, morning and evening every day, including Sunday.

I had a childhood experience of loving the Lord. But during my first two years in a large public high school I lost out spiritually. I was never guilty of outwardly doing anything contrary to the very high standards of our church or home. But in my heart I wanted to have my own way, and that means I was a sinner. You are not a sinner because of what you *do* outside, but because of what you *are* inside. As has often been said: When a ship's in the sea, it's safe; but when the sea's in the ship, it's sunk. And I had self-will inside. I was sunk.

Fortunately, my parents decided to send me away to a Quaker academy for my last two years of high school. Soon after I arrived there, in a Bible study class on Friday afternoon, I knelt beside my schoolroom chair, confessed I was nothing but a lowdown sinner, and asked Jesus to come into my heart as my Savior. He did, and my soul was flooded with joy. It was joy unspeakable and full of glory.

The next Monday morning in chapel the Holy Spirit convicted me of my need to be sanctified wholly. I knelt at the altar and asked God to fill my heart with His Holy Spirit.

This time there was a somewhat prolonged struggle before I could submit my will fully to God's will. I was faced with one thing that I felt I couldn't do.

I thought I had placed everything on the altar, to let God have His way with all my life. And then someone confronted me with a question that shook me: "Suppose God should ask you to preach on the Pullman car when you are going home next spring; would you do it?" (At that time I rode Pullman, with Dad paying the bills. When I paid the bills, I rode jalopy!)

I remembered that train ride out from Boston to Indianapolis. All the people in that Pullman car were nice, cultured, high-class adults. I could imagine getting up in front of that sophisticated group and starting to preach. No way! You'd never find this proud young Yankee from New England making a fool of himself doing that! I struggled at the altar in bitter tears.

Finally I became so desperate to be filled with the Spirit, that I cried out: "Yes, Lord, I'll do it if it kills me!" In that moment I died to self, and came fully alive in Christ. Emptied of self, I was filled with himself. I was as happy as a bird, and just as free.

I have made plenty of mistakes since that day, November 6, 1922. But I can honestly say that I never once have said no to God. Always my prayer has been: "Not my will, but yours be done" (Luke 22:42). That means perfect peace—and "a holy person." Now I could sing:

Peace! peace! wonderful peace,
  Coming down from the Father above!
Sweep over my spirit forever, I pray,
  In fathomless billows of love.

10

1 JOHN
Walking in the Light

"Walking in the beautiful light of God" is clearly portrayed in 1 John 1:7: "But if we walk in the light, as he is in the light, we have fellowship with one another, and the blood of Jesus, his Son, purifies us from all sin." The Greek word here is the same as that translated "all" in verse 9—"all unrighteousness."

What verse 7 declares is that if we walk in the light the blood of Jesus purifies (or "cleanses") us from *all* sin. That includes the sinful nature (inbred sin), as well as our sinful acts.

The main emphasis in 1 John is on "love." The Greek noun *agape* occurs 116 times in the New Testament. It is found most frequently (18 times) in the rather short First Epistle of John. It is the key word of this letter written by the beloved apostle in his old age. Incidentally, the Greek verb *agapao* ("love") is found most frequently in the Gospel of John (37 times) and his First Epistle (28 times)—65 out of the 142 times it occurs in the New Testament.

The fourth chapter, where we find the significant expression "perfect love," deserves special attention. In verse 12 John declares that "if we love one another, God lives in us and his love is made complete in us." Verse 17 says: "Love is made complete among us so that we will have confidence on the day of judgment." Finally, verse 18 tells us: "There is no fear in love. But perfect love drives out fear, because fear has to do with punishment. The one who fears is not made perfect in love."

The verb for "made complete" (vv. 12, 17) is *teleioo*, which comes from *telos*, "end." So it literally means "bring to an end," or "make complete." The adjective *perfect* (v. 18) is *teleia*, which means "complete" or "perfect." And *made perfect* (v. 18) is the same verb (slightly different form) as that translated "made complete" in verses 12 and 17. It does seem to us that it would be more consistent for the NIV to have "made perfect" in those two verses (cf. KJV, NASB).

As we have noted previously, "God is love" (1 John 4:8, 16), and the Holy Spirit is God. So when our hearts are "filled with the Holy Spirit" (Acts 2:4), they are filled with love—or, as John says, "made perfect in love." So the Spirit-filled Christian has the experience of "perfect love." John Wesley declared that his favorite designation of entire sanctification was "Christian perfection." In fact, his main book on the subject of sanctification is titled *Plain Account of Christian Perfection.*

One of the leading evangelical New Testament scholars of our day made an interesting observation. He wrote that for the Christian church Martin Luther rediscovered Paul, while John Wesley rediscovered John. Luther emphasized, especially from Romans, justification by faith. We are not saved by keeping the Mosaic law or church ordinances, but only by faith in Jesus Christ as Savior and Lord. Wesley, two centuries later, moved on to an emphasis on perfect love. And so the modern holiness movement came into existence in the 19th century and flourishes today. Of course Paul also gives considerable emphasis to the doctrine and experience of entire sanctification, as we have seen.

What has been emphasized throughout this book is that if we are going to be "filled with the Spirit" we must be "purified from all sin," including the "sinful nature" (carnality). In closing we should like to share one of the most vivid pictures of "the carnal mind" (as Paul designates it) to be found anywhere in literature. It occurs in C. S. Lewis's striking book *The Great Divorce.*

C. S. Lewis saw a man standing nearby, with a red lizard on his shoulder. This red lizard was a type of our inbred sin, or "sinful nature."

The lizard was talking into the man's ear. Lewis could tell by the look on the man's face that he was very much annoyed by the presence of the red lizard.

Just then Lewis saw "the Flaming Spirit"—his very appropriate designation for the Holy Spirit (see Matt. 3:11)—come near and say to the man, "Would you like me to make him quiet?"

"Yes!"

"Then I will kill him."

"No, I think the gradual process is better."

The Flaming Spirit answered: "The gradual process is of no use at all."

The man countered: "Some other day, perhaps."

The Flaming Spirit answered: "There is no other day." What a profound truth! God's Word declares: "Now is the day of salvation" (2 Cor. 6:2).

Then the man exclaimed: "Get back! You're burning me."

The Flaming Spirit replied: "I never said it wouldn't hurt you."

Then the man suggested: "Let me go back and get an opinion from my doctor. I'll come again the first moment I can."

Once more C. S. Lewis puts in the mouth of the Flaming Spirit a very striking statement: "This moment contains all moments." Each moment is a segment of eternity and can have eternal significance.

Then the man whined: "Why didn't you kill it without asking me?"

The Flaming Spirit answered: "I cannot kill it against your will. Have I your permission?"

"Do what you like; God help me."

The man screamed as the Burning One closed His crimson grip on the lizard, twisted it, and flung it dead at his feet.

Then C. S. Lewis writes these words: "There are only two kinds of people in the end: those who say to God, 'Thy will be done,' and those to whom God says, *'Thy* will be done'"— and that means hell, here on earth and forever in outer darkness.

Have you said that final, full yes to God: "Not my will, but Yours be done"? If you haven't, I would urge you right now to get down on your knees and say an everlasting "No!" to self and an everlasting "Yes!" to God. Then believe Him to sanctify you through and through.